The Job Survival Instruction Book

365 Tips, Tricks and Techniques to Stay Employed

By Karin Ireland

CAREER PRESS
180 Fifth Avenue—P.O. Box 34
Hawthorne, NJ 07507
1-800-CAREER-1   201-427-0229 (outside U.S.)
FAX: 201-427-2037

D1414098

THE JOB SURVIVAL INSTRUCTION BOOK ISBN 1-56414-133-0, $5.95. Cover design by
The Gottry Communications Group, Inc. Printed in the U.S.A. by Book-mart Press

To order this title by mail, please include price as noted above, $2.50 handling per order, and $1.00 for each book ordered. Send to: Career Press, Inc., 180 Fifth Ave., P.O. Box 34, Hawthorne, NJ 07507. Or call toll-free 1-800-CAREER-1 (Canada: 201-427-0229) to order using VISA or MasterCard, or for further information on books from Career Press.

Library of Congress Cataloging-in-Publication Data

Ireland, Karin.
      The job survival instruction book : 365 tips, tricks and techniques to stay employed / by Karin Ireland.
         p.   cm.
      Includes index.
      ISBN 1-56414-133-0 : $5.95
      1. Vocational guidance. 2. Vocational guidance--Quotations, maxims, etc. 3. Success in business--Quotations, maxims, etc. I. Title.
  HF5381.I64   1994
  650.14--dc20

                                         94-19989
                                             CIP

This book is dedicated to my daughter Tricia,
my friend, and my favorite first reader.

I'd like to express heartfelt thanks to Julie Castiglia, friend and agent extraordinaire—without her, this book wouldn't have happened; Peggy Sue Davis and Chris Lentz, co-walkers, co-workers, for years of laughs, endless offerings of Pic-N-Save gifts, and for taking precious time away from their families to pose for another Candid Communicator photo and offer valuable comments on this book; Lynda Leidiger, Connie Schimpf and Julie Edwards for making me feel welcome; Jerry Derloshon, for making it a pleasure to go to work; Tom Acosta and Cristi Saylor for their suggestions; and Betsy Sheldon for seeing the possibilities.

No one teaches us what we really need to know to get ahead in today's workplace. Schools teach us job skills and employers show us how to do the tasks and where to find the copy and coffee machines. Take it from someone who learned the hard way—that isn't enough.

It's possible to survive at work, even thrive and have fun...if you know how the game is played, if you know how to deal with the egos and the politics and if you understand the "obvious" rules that employees are expected to somehow know without being told.

This book is a collection of 365 practical tips for job success, some lighthearted, some serious, all true. Most are based on my personal experience, some are advice from others who make it their business to understand workplace dynamics. All are so simple you can put them to use instantly.

Whether you read this book to learn, to remember or to confirm that you're on the right track, whether you read a page or two at random or read it straight through, you'll find ideas you can use, right now, to be happier and more successful at work. And in real life, too.

Perfection is relative. Perfect for some tasks is creating an award-winning masterpiece. Perfect for others is just getting the job done.

Be decisive when you speak. Decisive people receive more attention and respect, even when they're wrong, than people who are right but sound uncertain.

The three most important parts of your job performance are attitude, attitude and attitude.

Go to meetings prepared and on time.

Do willingly the things your boss has the power and inclination to demand that you do.

Prioritize your work according to the 80/20 rule: Do the 20 percent that gives you 80 percent of the results.

When you're really sick, stay home. Nobody wants to catch what you've got.

Think before you ask questions; ask questions before you guess.

Specialize in something at work and be the best. *Someone* will, and you'll have more fun if it's you.

Establish personal boundaries that are comfortable for you and then gently, politely, but firmly, request that others honor them.

Do the best you can, then leave work and forget about it.

Say what you mean.
Mean what you say.
Do what you say you will do.

When the going gets tough, keep breathing. Deep, rhythmic breathing. Relax your jaw and shoulders and imagine being on a tropical beach.

Don't make a habit of working overtime. After a while, it will be expected and what you're able to do in a crunch will become what you're expected to do every day.

Understand what your boss wants from you and then give it to her.

No one feels confident or competent all the time. Fake it till you make it. Others will believe you're successful and, pretty soon, you will, too.

When people praise you for your brilliance, don't argue that you aren't. Simply smile, say thank you and be quiet.

Know the names and faces of your company's top executives.

Learn the fine art of saying little about things you know nothing about.

Meet deadlines by marking your calendar with the due date. Estimate how long each part of the project will take and move backwards on the calendar to set up a schedule.

Know your company's policy on personal use of the telephone, copy machine, fax machine and e-mail and follow it.

Prescription for workaholics: Do one fewer task a day than you think you have to or can.

Always tell the truth (but not necessarily all of it).

Don't drink the last cup of coffee without making more. If you do, don't admit it.

Proofread your paperwork before passing it on to someone else.

What goes around comes around. Keep that in mind or be ready to duck.

Management that doesn't have the time or money to do a job the way on-line workers say it should be done will find time and money to redo it when they discover you were right. Don't take it personally.

Anger that's hidden always comes out—usually at inappropriate times. Learn to communicate anger appropriately and as it occurs.

Never assume it's okay to swear, even if others do.

Three strategies for successful negotiation:

◊ Work to achieve your goal rather than to defend your position.

◊ Stick to the subject.

◊ Look for solutions where everyone wins.

Respond to the person, not the gestures, accents or habits that remind you of someone else.

Courtesy counts.

Set your watch ahead four minutes and forget you did it. You'll be surprised how much more often you arrive at work and at meetings on time.

When someone resists your ideas, ask questions before you try to explain the resistance away.

Whatever you believe, you achieve. With this law, you create both everything you want and everything you don't want.

Pursue balance in everything. Even in pursuing balance.

Don't feel you have to reinvent the wheel. When you're under deadline pressure, getting the job done is usually more important than finding a new or better way to do it.

Accept ownership for your good ideas—or others will.

When your boss suggests a change, agree enthusiastically to try it. If it doesn't work, you can always suggest going back to the old way.

When you make a complaint, know the resolution you want and ask for it.

The more you try to be in control, the less you really are...in life and at work.

Assertiveness is relative. Learn what's acceptable for each person and group and adjust your approach accordingly.

Never say anything at work you wouldn't want your co-workers and boss to hear.

Four words to eliminate:
- ◊ should
- ◊ shouldn't
- ◊ can't
- ◊ try

Quit smoking.

When you feel like you've hit bottom, pull yourself together—you probably haven't.

Don't believe everything you hear.
Don't believe everything you see.
Don't believe everything you're promised.

Employees who are helpful and easy to get along with are valued more than difficult people with better skills.

Timing is important. Know your boss. Approach him when he will be receptive.

Listen to the grapevine; it's usually at least partly right. Be discriminating about what you pass along.

Find a reason to laugh out loud at least twice a day. It's cheaper than therapy.

Learn as much about your company and its management as you can. When jobs are cut, who and what you know may determine whether you're asked to stay or go.

Avoid drinking around your boss. If pressured, nurse one for a long time.

Be willing to compromise on what you do and how you do it, but never compromise on what you believe and who you are.

Remember that you come first in your life. Also, remember that not everyone will share that view.

Don't argue to support your position; argue to find a solution.

Suppress the urge to confess your weaknesses. Confession doesn't make you look humble, it just makes you look weak.

Don't be fooled by a party atmosphere. Company get-togethers are not the place to relax and say what you really think of the company health plan, your workload or your boss's new haircut.

Put people (especially your boss) before paperwork. Put paperwork before socializing.

Respond, don't react, to people and situations.

Discourage drop-in visitors to your work area by keeping file folders on your chairs.

Four ways to appear more professional:

◊ Eliminate "uh," "um," "you know" and other fillers from your speech.
◊ Talk positively.
◊ Develop a firm speaking voice.
◊ Don't end statements with a question mark.

A messy desk is the sign of a busy person—unless there's dust on the top layer of papers.

Don't borrow money from your co-workers.
Don't borrow money from your boss.
Don't lend money to either.

Ask a good friend to let you know if you have bad breath. If you do, consult a dentist and carry breath mints.

Make an arrangement with a co-worker to signal you when you have green food stuck in your teeth or clothes tags flapping in the breeze.

If a project seems overwhelming, break it into several steps. Reward yourself each time you complete a step.

Accept the fact that when you wear your white suit or your best silk tie to work, it will be the day your lunch friends want to go out for spaghetti.

Enlist others as allies in your mission.

Never complain about your boss to your co-workers. Never ever complain about your boss to someone in another department. And never complain about your boss to your boss.

Before you leave work, have a clear idea of what you want to accomplish the next day and what you'll do first.

It's less important to get everything done than it is to get the most important things done.

Look for ways a job can be done instead of reasons why it can't.

Celebrate the differences between people.

Don't plan your wedding, open house, vacation or best friend's baby shower on company time. Co-workers hate hearing you have time to plan something fun while they're struggling to get the work done...especially if they're doing your work.

Commit 100 percent to what you're doing each moment.

Notice the silent conversations you have with yourself. If they're negative, change the subject to something positive.

When you write, write the way you talk and not to please your old high school English teacher.

When someone asks how you are, unless it's your mother or your therapist, just say, "Great."

Keep a victory log and write down every time you meet a goal, keep a commitment or find a win-win solution to a problem.

Know your company's mission.
Know *your* mission.

Know your company's competition.
Know *your* competition.

Know your company's fears.
Know *your* fears.

Never involve yourself in office politics that don't feel honest to you.

Take inventory often: Is what you're doing getting you where you want to go at work? Is your job getting you where you want to go in *life?*

Before you do anything, know your goal. Before you start a project, make a phone call, ask a question, write a memo or make a decision—know the result you want or need then determine the steps necessary to reach it.

When talking to your boss, stick to the point; be pleasant, but brief.

Accept competition when it excites you; avoid competition when it causes you to feel anxious and angry.

Bring your own coffee mug to work; it makes you feel more at home.

When you're in the right job you don't have to struggle to succeed.

When you're asked to do something you don't know how to do, don't panic. Nod confidently, leave calmly and find someone who does know how to do it.

Be willing to show up at work on time.

The purpose of the company newsletter is to pass along messages from upper management. Newsletters generally tell the truth but they aren't obligated to print all of it.

Show respect for your fellow workers, whether they deserve it or not.

When you leave a company for another job, leave on a positive note. It could be helpful someday for your boss and co-workers to remember you kindly.

If you have a bad day at work, do something to break that mood before you go home to your family. Listen to some nice music, eat chocolate, go shopping, meditate, eat chocolate, take a walk or eat chocolate.

Avoid fighting other people's battles.

Ask what you can learn about yourself from people and situations at work that annoy you.

Change happens. It isn't always for the best but employees who accept it without complaining are appreciated and sometimes even rewarded.

Accept that if your boss thinks something is important, it is.

Four strategies for surviving change:
- ◊ Cooperate with whomever is in charge.
- ◊ Appear positive and optimistic.
- ◊ Learn about the goals of those in charge.
- ◊ Do what you can to help them reach those goals.

Always keep your resume updated.

Take your rest breaks and don't talk about work. (If you talk about work, it's not a break.)

It takes just as much energy to be nasty as it takes to be nice. Nasty may feel better at times, but nice will get you further.

Be careful what you wish for; you just might get it.

You can always decide to go back and say something to a boss, co-worker, employee later, but you can never *unsay* something said.

Be patient with everybody—including yourself.

Begin conflict resolution by asking what the other person thinks before saying what you think. After he's said what's on his mind, he'll be more likely to listen to you.

Do the work you love. If you can't, do what you love as a hobby. You may get a job by being in the right place at the right time.

Always have neat, clean fingernails.

If you don't ask for something you'll never know if you could have gotten it.

Five more ways to appear more professional:

◊ Notice and eliminate nervous habits.
◊ Dress as nicely as you can afford to.
◊ Act confident (even you aren't).
◊ Look people in the eye.
◊ Play by your boss's and your company's rules.

Interrupt conversations with co-workers to help customers and clients.

Anytime you argue with a customer, you lose. Even if you win, you lose.

People can generally recognize when you're in a bad mood but they appreciate a warning before you snap.

Information is power. Learn how and where people get it in your company.

Keep your boss updated on the status of your projects.

Use your best manners at meals even though you're just at work.

Don't take yourself too seriously.

Never ridicule anyone, even as a joke, even to make a point, even if he or she laughs, too.

Don't try to change the system unless it's discriminatory or dangerous. It was there before you were and something is keeping it there. Instead, learn how to make it work for you.

If you believe you're a victim of sexual, racial, age or religious discrimination or abuse, tell your boss. If he or she is unwilling or unable to help, tell the next person up the line of command.

Most people will treat you the way you expect to be treated.

Bosses never quite get their thoughts in order until after you've typed the final draft. Accept this or it will make you crazy.

Question authority, but question it to yourself until you have some authority.

The Golden Rule is still a good idea.

It's usually easier to go *around* a barrier than through it.

When you want something done, go directly to the person who can get it done.

Waiting until everything is perfect before making a move is like waiting to start a trip until all the traffic lights are green.

Be the kind of person others enjoy having around.

Always listen with the possibility that the person who's talking could be right. Even when you're dead sure she's wrong.

Try not to be sick on Fridays or Mondays. No one will believe you.

Don't appear desperate at a job interview.

Acknowledge people, especially your boss, quickly when they enter your workspace.

Comparing yourself or your work to other people is a no-win exercise. Compare yourself only to your own best.

Never be late to a job interview. If you absolutely can't help it, apologize simply and have a really good excuse.

Decide to be happy each day.

Congratulate yourself every day for five things you did well. Little things count as much as big things.

In communication, listening is generally more important than talking.

Laws protect minority and disabled employees. Help make the world a place where those laws aren't needed.

Set up five daily goals. Carry over what you don't finish to the next day.

Don't make promises you can't keep.

Eliminate negative body language that can give you away: tapping fingers, rolling eyes, arms locked across chest, looking away from the speaker, clenched teeth, fidgeting.

When making decisions, weigh the facts, then pay attention to your gut feeling.

Be organized. Write things down. Make "to do" lists, schedule meetings and deadlines, and document papers you send and receive.

Three tips for answering the phone:

◊ Don't challenge callers to give more information than they want to.
◊ Don't sound suspicious or bored.
◊ Write down the name the first time you hear it.

Join Toastmasters. You'll learn how to speak in front of others and, although the butterflies might not go away, you'll learn how to make them fly in formation.

The perfect job is something you'd do even if nobody paid you.

Show up with donuts for the gang occasionally. Don't do it regularly, though, or people will resent it when you don't.

Never let your boss see you take a magazine to the restroom.

Keep at least three months' salary in a savings account. If you lose your job unexpectedly, it could take you that long to find another one.

Generally you can act a little nicer than you feel, but only a *little* nicer. If you try to be a saint, you'll find yourself smiling with clenched teeth.

Most co-workers will be happy to hear about your great weekend. *Once.*

Know your goals: To do, to have, to be. Review them every day. Say them out loud for the best results.

Notice that what you think about and talk about is what shows up in your job and in your life.

Don't expect yourself to be perfect. When you make a mistake, don't make excuses. Don't try to explain it away, just learn from it and go on.

Be good to every living thing—starting with yourself.

Get a new job offer in writing before you quit your present job or say no to other potential employers.

Avoid "us vs. them" comments.

Don't yell at your boss, even if he or she yells at you. It's okay to ask for a break until you both cool down.

Keep learning: Work a crossword puzzle, read news magazines, borrow kids' nonfiction books (they're short and to the point) from the library.

Tell co-workers when you hear something good about them.

Don't get so busy *doing* that you forget about *being*—being happy, being patient, being kind.

Someone who starts a sentence with, "I'm going to be perfectly honest with you," probably isn't.

It isn't enough to be valuable if the right people don't know that you are. Make yourself noticeable in positive ways.

Let your boss know what you need to succeed, and if you're the boss, provide your employees with what *they* need to succeed.

Nothing can get you as far as good self-esteem. If you don't have it, learn how to develop it. If you do have it, work to increase it.

Strive to be curious rather than right.

Don't let things build up. If you have a problem with a co-worker, ask to talk about it and find a solution that works for both of you.

Approximate truth sometimes paints a more accurate picture than telling the absolute facts.

Don't sign anything you haven't read.

When people help you, express your thanks and then surprise them by asking what you can do for them.

If you're anything less than 100 percent committed to your present job, keep it to yourself.

Don't let your boss make you feel guilty. Do your best and let it go.

Warning: Complaining is habit-forming and may be hazardous to your health.

Your boss will like your ideas better if you find a way to let her think they're hers.

Act—don't react. There's no law that says you have to answer questions or respond to criticisms from your boss or co-workers on the spot. Take time, if you need it, to separate your feelings from the message and form a response.

Never give anyone the only copy of important paperwork.

Work to be good, not perfect.

Management doesn't always do what is reasonable or fair. Management doesn't appreciate having junior employees tell them that what they're doing isn't reasonable or fair.

Develop a sense of humor. It's better to laugh than to cry and sometimes those will be your only two options.

Avoid office romances. They're distracting when they work and painful when they don't.

Everyone wants to feel special. You can be special if you help others feel that they are.

People will want you to be perfect. You may believe that you should be perfect. You can't be. But nobody else can, either.

It's usually easier to get forgiveness than it is to get permission.

Don't interrupt, even when you already know what the other person is going to say and you know that what you have to say is more clever or important.

Four ways to reduce stress:

◊ Get some physical exercise every day.
◊ Find people to laugh with.
◊ Be around people who are positive.
◊ Work where there is something besides money that is positive about your job.

What you say may not be what the other person hears. What you hear may not be what the other person means. Check it out.

People don't always want advice, sometimes they only want you to listen and agree that they're right.

At work and in life, you get what you look for.

When you're frustrated, ask yourself if it will matter in 10 years, and if not, take a deep breath and let it go.

A job interview is not the place to share anything radical or extreme about yourself, no matter how interesting you think it is.

Give your inner critic a name and tell it to be quiet.

Get to know the culture of your company by looking at the leaders. The more you appear to be like the leaders, the better your chances are for success.

Always believe the impossible is possible.

Be positive. What you say and think determines how you feel. How you feel determines what you do. What you do determines what you have.

Life is a journey, not a destination. Be gentle with yourself when you hit bumps in the road. A lot of those bumps will be at work.

Stress buster: Today, only think about things that you need to make a decision on today.

Wear name tags on your right side, where people naturally look when they shake your hand.

No matter what you do, you won't be able to please everybody all the time. That's okay. Just do your best.

Listening attentively is the most sincere form of flattery.

Go outside at lunch time, especially if you work in an air-conditioned office, with computer screens, fluorescent lights and other unnatural conditions.

Never doubt that the difficult can be done.

Post or circulate a cute cartoon strip for co-workers to enjoy.

Never disclose information told to you in confidence—even if you weren't asked not to tell.

You'll enjoy your job more if you work for the fun things you can do with your money instead of the bills you're going to pay.

Find the right occupation. Find the right company. You'll know when you're there by the way you feel.

Know the customs of your foreign customers and clients and be sensitive to their preferences.

Learn the difference between being assertive and being aggressive.

Sales tip: Smile when you dial the phone. Then talk as if you were talking to a friend.

If you keep doing things the way you're doing them now, you'll keep getting the same results. To see changes in what you get, you need to change what you do.

Never help someone with the punch line of a joke. Never help your boss with any part of a joke.

Practice putting yourself in the other person's shoes.

Everyone is in sales. Learn how to sell yourself, your ideas, your value.

Demonstrate your power as confidence and inner calm instead of outward bravado.

Don't mumble.
Don't whine.
Don't cheat on your expense reports.

There's an old saying, "Don't shoot the messenger." In job talk, that means don't be angry with your boss if he passes along bad news from *his* boss.

Do the job you were hired to do and then volunteer for other duties if you have time.

Put some money in a savings account every payday.

Life is supposed to be fun. If you have a bad day, decide to have a good day tomorrow.

Surround yourself with the brightest, sharpest people you can find. Generally, you're known by the company you keep.

Sandwich criticism between two genuine compliments.

Don't make decisions based on the experience of others.

Don't let anyone at work know you're looking for another job. If your boss finds out, you might be leaving sooner than you planned.

If you can't explain your idea in a couple of minutes, you probably aren't ready to explain it.

Five things job interviewers want to know:

◊ Why you think you can do the job.
◊ How well you will fit in with the current staff.
◊ How skilled you are.
◊ How willing you are to work.
◊ Why you should be chosen over other applicants.

Identify someone at your company who is well-informed and become friends.

If you look for sympathy, you'll probably get it. Look for answers and you're more likely to solve the problem.

It may be unfair, but people judge you by the way you look. Do the best with what you have.

Don't upstage your boss.

Evaluate your behavior/performance regularly to see if you're on track but learn to turn off your internal critic (the voice that tells you you're not measuring up no matter what you do).

Replace scuffed briefcases, worn or dirty purses, rundown heels.

Let others own their behavior. Don't assume that if your boss, a co-worker or client is in a bad mood it's your fault.

Own your own behavior. Don't blame others for your bad mood.

Be nice to your boss even if you don't like him. Ask yourself what you can learn from the situation. If it's intolerable, look for a new job.

Tell the secretary why you're calling her boss—don't play games.

People will respect you more if you let them feel great when they're with you than if you try to convince them how great you are.

Write down three things you'd like to be known for, decide how you can make that happen and then take action.

When others complain about a co-worker, change the subject.

Follow your dream, but don't quit your day job until you can support yourself.

Take notes when your boss gives you instructions. Ask her to slow down and repeat if you don't understand.

Don't make a big deal out of a little thing.

Everyone has his or her own view of reality. Don't take it personally when other people don't share yours.

Don't take things—even little things—from work. It's stealing.

Honor your company's corporate philosophy. If you can't, look for a new job.

People who are positive and fun attract people who are positive and fun, and they can soften people who are grumpy.

Start each project with enthusiasm and finish it on time.

Even when you fail in a project, you are not a failure. Don't let yourself think you are or you'll convince others, too.

When overwhelmed by too much work, ask your boss to suggest which jobs are a priority.

If you don't have anything to do, find something to do.

Use bias-free language. Don't tell insensitive jokes and don't laugh when others do.

Don't agree to work at a company where you feel uncomfortable with the people you meet or the things you see and hear.

Don't spend more time and energy making a decision than it's worth.

Don't waste your time over-analyzing whether the decision you made was right.

Write thank-you notes after job interviews and be sure to spell the interviewer's name right.

Job interviewers like applicants with ambition, enthusiasm and confidence.

Honesty isn't the best policy if you feel your boss is a jerk.

Think of your job as a game. There are strategies that can lead to success and traps that can cost you. Take time to learn the rules.

Remember some of the positive aspects of your job each day on your way home from work.

Be known as a source of chocolate and other goodies.

Don't let authoritarian co-workers and bosses trigger old parent-child or sibling emotions. Learn to detach what's happening in the present from what happened in the past.

Never say anything negative at a job interview. Not about your last job, your last employer, your commute to the interview or even your dog. Questions that try to draw negative answers from you may be a test.

Generally, people believe about you what you believe about yourself.

Be nice to everyone. Today's administrative assistant could be tomorrow's leader.

Know which tasks your boss feels are most important. Do these with care and high visibility.

Share information, but don't share all your sources.

Carrying a grudge at work is like carrying a sack of hand grenades. Unproductive and potentially dangerous.

Take time from doing to think—but if your employer pays you only to *do*, it might be better to think on your own time.

Five power tips for presenting information:

◊ Know who is the decision-maker.
◊ Know what you want the decision-maker to think and feel after your presentation.
◊ Determine what information you must present to accomplish that result.
◊ Use eye contact with key players.
◊ Act comfortable.

Work off stress with 20 minutes of physical exercise.

Don't assume that if your boss doesn't complain about something she doesn't notice or mind.

Leave your gum at home.

Pass along helpful information. Don't hoard information as a means of control.

Give someone the benefit of the doubt twice. Then be suspicious.

When you've found the perfect solution to a problem, keep looking until you've found a few more. Choosing one from several gives you a greater opportunity for success.

Never smell food left in containers in the lunchroom refrigerator to see if it's bad. If in doubt, throw it out.

Throw out leftover food before it gets fuzzy.

People are promoted for two reasons: because they appear to have good job skills and because it appears they will fit in.

Look for ways to save your manager and your company time and money.

Volunteer to do jobs you don't mind doing anyway.

Identify your weaknesses. Work on correcting them and don't talk about it while you do.

Success comes from working smart, not hard. Prioritize your tasks; pay attention to what you're doing so you don't make mistakes; don't waste time at work doing things that aren't job related.

Accept it: No job is perfect all the time.

When someone makes a rude comment, calmly say, "Excuse me, would you repeat that please?" Give her a chance to rethink.

At most companies if you're not willing to be part of the solution, you're part of the problem.

Listen to music on the way to work instead of news.

Rehearse difficult situations. Prepare for difficult questions and objections and practice answering them.

Don't get hooked on proving you're a hard worker by passing up coffee breaks. Bosses usually don't notice and it actually reduces your productivity.

Be unemotional when criticizing someone. Be specific and do it in private.

Protect yourself by telling others you need information or supplies a day or two before you really do. But don't pad your deadlines excessively.

Network now. Once you need those contacts it's too late to start.

Go to work on days when you're just a little bit sick. Save a few sick-pay days to take when you're well enough to enjoy them.

Handle each piece of paper only once. If you can act on it without additional information, do.

Don't take telephone calls you can postpone when you're working on a deadline.

Be flexible.

Job security comes not only from doing your job well but from helping your boss achieve his goals, too.

Don't skip breakfast.

Don't skip lunch.

Remember that if you don't ask for what you want you'll get what others want to give you.

Visualize the results you want, not the ones you fear.

People tend to remember the first and last blocks of information in a series and forget what's in the middle. Take breaks when you're learning new material so you create firsts and lasts. Write memos with three or less points.

You won't get everything you ask for. Don't take it personally. Don't stop asking.

If it seems too good to be true, it probably is.

Misery loves company and if you listen to others' problems too often or too long, you'll be miserable too.

Be a problem-solver.

Four more power tips for presenting information:

◊ Introduce your point.
◊ Give your facts.
◊ Draw your conclusion.
◊ Ask for action.

When you feel you absolutely must take action, stop. Wait until the urgency to act has passed. After a while, if you still believe taking action is right, then do it.

Don't be pressured into signing rosters for information or training you didn't receive.

Only people who don't do anything don't make any mistakes.

Your body language and your tone of voice say more than your words.

From time to time ask a trusted work friend to let you know what kind of impression you're making.

Read a different magazine each week just to see what's out there.

Go out of your way to make the new person feel welcome. It will make both of you feel good, and you can't have too many allies.

No one can give you authority. But if you act like you have it, others will believe you do.

People with high confidence and low skills are given more recognition and opportunities to advance than people with low confidence and high skills.

Ask permission from your telephone caller before putting him or her on hold.

When you tell your boss about a problem, have a few solutions
to suggest.

Never say anything at work you wouldn't want to see printed
in *People* magazine.

If you want to know what you believe, look at what you've
created in your life.

Often, being a good listener will get your further than being a good talker.

Don't whine and don't spend time with people who do.

You don't have to like everyone you have lunch with. Lunches with people who can share important information are as important as lunches with people you like.

Bosses are moody.
Co-workers are moody.
When you're moody, try not to take it out on your boss and co-workers.

Work is an important part of your life but it's only part of it. Be sure to also include friends, fun, giving and spiritual growth.

Practice taking criticism gracefully. Go to the restroom and grit your teeth later if you have to.

Ignore trivial things you can't control. If you can't ignore them, at least keep quiet about them.

Don't fight to win the battle if it means you'll lose the war.

Treat the boss like a good guy—even if he isn't.

Notice what time of the day you're most energetic and enthusiastic. Try to do your most demanding work then.

Generally, good work is taken for granted and only the errors will be mentioned. Don't wait for applause from your boss to feel good.

Sometimes it takes years for a good idea to be recognized for the gem it is. Don't give up.

A trick to help you remember the order of points in a talk is to mentally assign a point to each finger. As you speak, keep your place by resting the correct finger on the lectern, the table or your lap.

Tell a story once, twice if you must, and then retire it.

Set a timed deadline for every task. Challenge yourself to beat the clock.

Old rule for successful talks:
  Tell 'em what you're going to tell 'em.
  Tell 'em.
  Tell 'em what you told 'em.

Have fun at work every day. You spend more time at work than anyplace else so you might as well enjoy it.

You will usually be your own worst enemy. Look for ways you might be sabotaging yourself.

People won't always do what you want them to but if they like you, they'll go along most of the time.

If you can't spell, look words up or use a spell-check program.

Four types of people and how to win them over:

Controllers prefer to be in charge of people and events. Give them facts quickly and clearly. Let them know what to expect.

Promoters enjoy the challenge of setting projects in motion. Help them find ways to solve problems and overcome challenges.

Analyzers prefer to question and analyze issues from all sides. Give them facts and be patient, but set realistic deadlines for responses.

Supporters are comfortable supporting others. Let them know they are important. Support them by listening and appreciating their efforts.

Notice how your boss prefers to get information and use that style. Some prefer to hear only the bottom line, others want to chat first. When in doubt, ask the secretary. If you are the secretary, ask your boss.

People don't resent things they have to do. They resent doing things they weren't honest enough to say they didn't want to do.

Listen a lot. Smile a lot. Forgive a lot.

You can hide from office politics but you can't escape them. Learning how they work at your job can make the difference between sweet success and sudden death.

When you're telling a story and your listener interrupts with, "You already told me that," take the hint.

Don't tell everyone how people did things at your old company. Unless you were hired to make changes, wait until you prove yourself before you suggest new procedures.

Talk to a financial advisor even if you don't think you have much money—*especially* if you don't have much money. What you earn won't determine your financial future as much as what you do with what you earn.

Welcome the unexpected. It will come anyway, and the more positive you are about it, the more successful you'll be in dealing with it.

Something done with passion is more likely to succeed than something done out of duty.

Need to be intuitive? Creative? Cover your left nostril and breathe through your right. Need to be logical? Cover your right nostril and breathe through the left.

Good employees are not necessarily good supervisors. If you are promoted, get training—at your company or outside—for the role.

When negotiating a salary or asking for a raise, ask for more than you want. You can always come down but you can never go up.

Remember to say "please" and "thank you."

Three steps to success:

◊ Identify a skill you admire.

◊ Find out how you can learn it.

◊ Do what it takes to get it.

Work isn't the place to brag about your sexual conquests.

In the information-swap business, you have to give to get. Tuck a few trades in the back of your mind that are important, but that don't betray confidences. And don't tell everything you know.

Look for others' hidden agendas. It's okay for them to be there, but it's to your benefit to know what they are.

Be aware of your hidden agendas.

It's human nature to want to edit, rewrite or change what others write and say. Don't take it personally if your boss red-pens your communications.

People ask for advice when they don't want to do what they know they should do. Be sympathetic and let them figure it out for themselves.

Be nice to secretaries and assistants. Most have information you don't have. Some will hint or tell you about it, all have their boss's ear.

Make yourself indispensable.

Take the time to make those special gestures that show people you care—give your *own* birthday card instead of just signing the department card.

Don't apologize unless it's your fault. Saying, "I'm sorry," when someone is upset can link you, in his or her mind, to the source of that upset whether or not you were involved.

Remove anything from your appearance that identifies you with a group or beliefs, unless everyone shares it. In other words, take off the "Young Republicans" button, unless you're at a Young Republican's meeting.

In the scramble to do and have, it's easy to forget to *be*—to be gentle with yourself and others, to be pleased with small successes, to be happy in the moment.

You will probably forget a lot of this. Read the book again.